MAKING EARLY PERCUSSION INSTRUMENTS

Early Music Series: 3

MAKING EARLY
PERCUSSION INSTRUMENTS

JEREMY MONTAGU

OXFORD UNIVERSITY PRESS

MUSIC DEPARTMENT
44 CONDUIT STREET, LONDON WIR ODE

Printed in Great Britain
by The Stellar Press Hatfield
Hertfordshire

CONTENTS

mus/bur

4.4.85

5 MISCELLANEOUS

LIST OF FIGURES

LIST OF PLATES

To Jimmy Blades,
best of teachers, mentor, and friend
with all gratitude

PREFACE

For many years, players of early music have gone to great trouble to re-create early string, wind, and keyboard instruments but have been content to accompany these with whatever drums came to hand. When I first began to play with Musica Reservata, I felt that this was wrong; that the percussion instruments were as important as any of the others and that it was just as important to obtain the correct sonorities on the percussion instruments as on the melodic. Unfortunately, there is far less surviving evidence to help the drummer than there is for the other players. No early percussion instruments have come down to us. All that we have is the work of the sculptors, the painters, the drawers, and the illuminators of manuscripts. The illustrations are mute; they can never come to life and reveal the sound of early music, but they can show us the appearance of the instruments and we can say, with absolute certainty, that if we use an instrument that looks wrong, it cannot possibly sound right.

I believe that we should reconstruct early percussion instruments as nearly like artists' illustrations of them as possible, calling upon all our knowledge of modern drum construction and of the methods used elsewhere in the world to fill the gaps in our information, to help us to reconstruct the details which the artists did not show. Having done this, we can say that the instruments look right; perhaps, and with luck, they may sound right. At least we have done what we can and at least we know that we are nearer to the truth than we would be if we continued to use modern instruments or to hit any old drum.

In that spirit, this book is offered to my colleagues who may also wish for greater authenticity in percussion. It is a companion to *Early Percussion Instruments*, written by James Blades and myself. It is a necessary book because, to my knowledge, so far only one professional maker, Paul Williamson of Crowland, has used what I have learned in fifteen years of early drum making, in order to make instruments of a better quality than mine. My readers can make for themselves, if they are inclined to the craft, or else they can encourage others to make for them. Whichever course they choose, they should read with special attention the sections dealing with lapping and stitching drum heads, for all drummers, whether of old or of modern music, should be able to carry out their own repairs and to replace broken drum heads in emergencies.

N.B. 2.5cm. equals one inch, 15cm. is approximately six inches.

INTRODUCTION

As has been said in the Preface and in *Early Percussion Instruments*, no drums or other percussion instruments have survived from earlier than the sixteenth century, at least so far as concerns our music of the Middle Ages and Renaissance. The result is that we look at all the iconographic representations that we can find, we try to scale the instruments from the bodies of the players and we apply all the knowledge that we possess of European and non-European drum construction to fill in the details missing from the pictures and carvings. However authentic we are trying to be, modern concert-giving conditions must also exert an influence. In the Middle Ages, as in much folk music today, if a drum were getting slack, there was no reason why one should not stop playing, wander over to the fireplace and hold the drum over the fire until the heads had tightened again. Today, the modern audience expects one to go on playing whatever happens and drums which need not have had adjustable tension in their own time must now be adjustable without the use of heat. Snares must also be adjustable, but there is no medieval authority for the method suggested below; it has been taken from the modern Basque tabor. It is simple, effective, and could have been used in the Middle Ages, which applies also to the method chosen for tensioning the skins. Few early pictures show any form of tensioning; those that do, show ropes of some sort. The Vs of rope with sliding buffs, familiar to us from the military drum, were certainly in use by about 1500 and may have been used earlier.

An experienced craftsman should be able to construct drum shells. The less skilled, like the author, will rely upon modern drums which can be modified and converted. A small tabor can be made from an old jazz Chinese tom-tom, for example, or from the small side drums made for young school children, though care should be taken to ensure that such shells will be sufficiently strong. My largest tabor was made from two tenor tom-tom shells glued together; such instruments must be stripped of their fittings, have all the holes plugged with dowel and be painted in some less modern style. A small, Dürer-size side drum (see p.8 in *Early Percussion Instruments*) can be made from a cylindrical bongo. A large side drum, of the size described by Arbeau, can be made by fixing together two thirty-inch-diameter and fifteen-inch-deep military bass drums. But a thirty-by-thirty-inch side drum, however authentic, may be larger than the doors of the car in which the drums will be transported, and an instrument of more moderate size can be made from a 56cm. jazz bass drum. A Handelian side drum could be made from a tenor tom-tom, but it would be necessary to have wooden counter hoops made because the metal hoops that are fitted on such drums today are unsuitable for rope tensioning. Timbrels can be made from modern tambourines by removing the jingles and replacing them with new ones, made as described below. (See plates 5, 6 and 7.)

Whether the reader intends to make shells or to convert pre-existing ones, it would be wise to look first at a modern side drum, to see how it is made and to identify the constituent parts. A drum with a wooden shell (for this is the material that will be used), and with plastic heads, so that the interior can be seen through the lower head, is the most suitable. Fig. a gives the names of most of the parts of a drum and is shown as rope-tensioned for future reference.

The body is normally referred to as the shell. Note that there is an air hole in the side of the shell. Note that the snares, the coils of spring wire on the modern drum (gut on the older instruments) which give the rattling sound characteristic of the side drum, lie in a bed; if the shell were not shaved down at these points, the snare would stand proud of the drum head and would not rattle against it. Note that the shell is quite thin but is supported by internal rings of wood at each end of the shell, shaped so that only their outermost edges touch the skin. Note that there are two hoops at each end, one with the skin fixed to it, the flesh hoop, the other, the counter hoop, holding the flesh hoop on the drum. Passing through holes in the counter hoop are either metal rods or ropes, whose tension can be adjusted so as to tighten or slacken the tension of the heads.

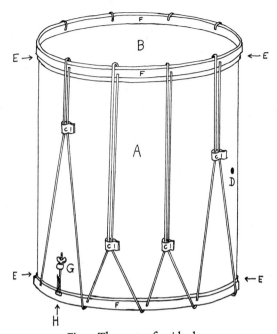

Fig. a The parts of a side drum
(a) the shell; (b) the batter head; (c) the buffs; (d) the air hole; (e) the flesh hoop; (f) the counter hoop; (g) the snare tension control; (h) the snare channel

This is essential because a slack head gives a dull sound and calf skin is extremely hygroscopic, so that continual adjustment is essential. Plastic 'skin' is not affected in this way but is of no use to us because it would falsify the sound; the tone quality is quite different from that of calf. The metal rods are tightened by screwing them into sockets; ropes are tightened by drawing the Vs together by moving leather buffs down from the apex of each V. The snares are tensioned by a screw device, usually combined today with a quick-release lever. Finally, there is a head on each end of the drum, the upper one, the one that is struck, known as the batter head, the lower called the snare head.

We will now consider the construction of the various types of drum. It is emphasised that because some drums require fittings that are not needed on others, this book is not arranged as a step-by-step construction manual. It is essential to read the first three chapters before starting work.

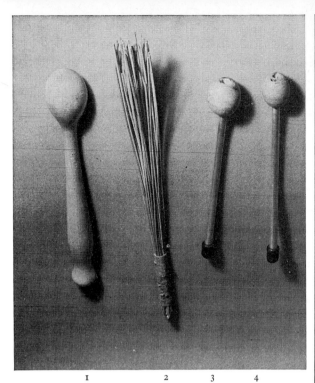

I   2   3   4

Plate 1 Beaters: (1)
Solid beater; (2) Switch
for the Long Drum;
(3 and 4) Tabor beaters
made of aluminium
tubing and plumber's
bobs; (5) Tabor beater
by Paul Williamson;
(6) Beater in aluminium;
(7 and 8) Longer beaters
commercially available
in nylon and wood

Plate 2 (*far right*)
Jingling Johnnie. Repro-
duced by courtesy of
Tony Bingham

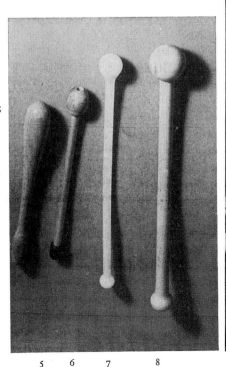

5   6   7   8

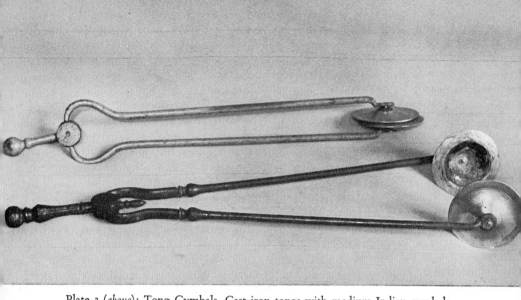

Plate 3 (*above*): Tong Cymbals. Cast iron tongs with medium Indian cymbals

Plate 4 (*below*): Normal chamber timpani (lower) and Double Drums (upper) with reproductions of various early timpani sticks

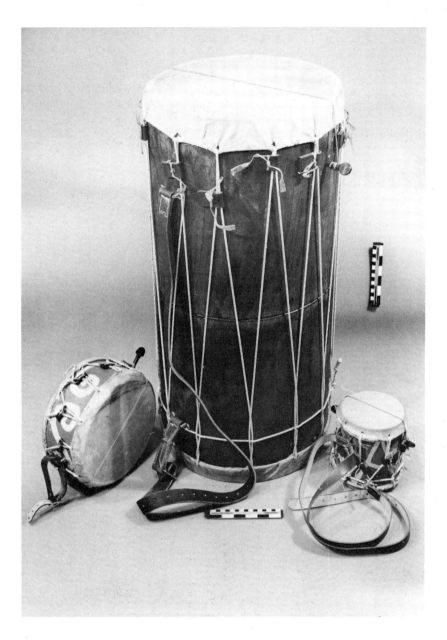

Plate 5: Small Tabor made from Chinese tomtom shell; Deep Tabor made from two tenor tomtom shells; Small Side Drum, after Dürer.

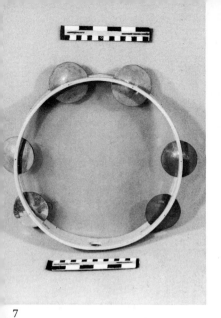

7

6

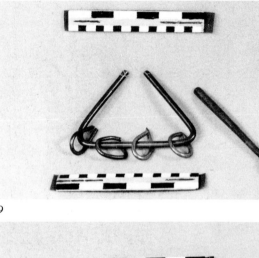

9

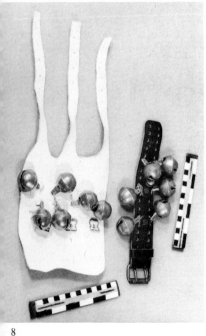

8

10

Plate 6: Pair of Nakers made from copper mixing bowls.

Plate 7: Timbrel made from commercial tambourine.

Plate 8: Pellet Bells on wrist straps.

Plate 9: Triangle and beater.

Plate 10: Chinese Cymbals.

I

THE SHELLS

TABOR AND SIDE DRUM

To make the shell for a tabor or side drum, a sheet of wood is needed of sufficient area to produce a cylinder of the right size plus a good overlap. The seventeenth-century side drum in the Tower of London, which is 56cm. in diameter, has an overlap of more than 15cm. and it is likely that even a drum of the Dürer size, about 15cm. in diameter, would have had 6 or 7cm. of overlap. Modern side drums have a very short overlap, consisting of a diagonal, glued scarfe joint (fig. b). The Tower drum has an overlap of a double thickness of wood and the joint is held by an ornamental pattern of nails (fig. c), such as can be seen in Rembrandt's painting of 'The Night Watch'; the nails are driven through from the outside and turned over inside. Once the diameter of the drum has been decided, this must be multiplied by π ($3\frac{1}{7}$ is near enough for most purposes). The result plus the length of the overlap gives the length of the sheet of wood required; the width of the sheet is the depth of the drum. Dimensions of various tabors and side drums are given in *Early Percussion Instruments* (and an illustration of the Tower Drum, on p.11) but to recapitulate briefly, the following were suggested: Tabors 25cm. diam. by 10cm. deep; 40cm. by 80cm.; 30cm. by 40cm. Side drums 15cm. by 15cm.; 75-80cm. by 75-80cm.; 41cm by 38cm.

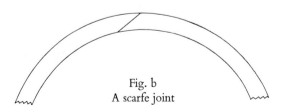

Fig. b
A scarfe joint

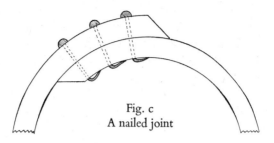

Fig. c
A nailed joint

The Tower side drum is made from a sheet of oak 3mm. thick, about 49.5cm. wide by just over 180cm. long. Today, plywood is a more easily obtainable material than 3mm. oak, but if thin wood can be obtained it would be better to follow the original practice and have all the grain running round the drum instead of the plywood construction of some grain running round and some across. Ash is often used today, and chestnut is another wood used historically. A long-grain ply could be made up by wrapping and gluing thin sheets of veneer round a cylindrical former until the required thickness has been built up. The normal method of bending wood is by steaming it, and a fair amount of patience, steam, and space is required, for if one works too fast, the wood is likely to crack and split. The drum shell must be cylindrical (if it is not, the tone will suffer) and it must therefore be bent round a cylindrical former. This can either be a solid block, if anything of suitable size is available or can be turned up, or it may be made by joining two or more discs with slats to make a hollow cylinder. With this latter method, the discs must be smaller than the interior diameter of the drum by two thicknesses of slat. If the shell is built up from veneer, it can be held on the former while the glue cures with webbing straps or with ropes; some method of tightening the straps or ropes, such as a tourniquet, will be necessary because either will stretch over the period that most glues require. Wedges should not be used lest they dent the shell. An ornamental nail pattern can then be added as a decorative feature if desired.

An alternative method of bending up a shell, without the use of steam or a former, will be found clearly explained in Picken's description of the construction of the Turkish davul. This requires the use of a wood-bending mangle (Picken, fig. 6) but, if a domestic clothes mangle could be adapted, might well prove a simpler method. Much other useful information will be found in this book on Turkish folk instruments.

Strengthening rings must be fitted inside the ends of the shell. A head pulls more strongly in one direction than the other, and, without such rings, the drum would soon be oval. Modern strengthening rings are thick and are joined with a scarfe joint. The strengthening rings on the Tower side drum are of wood 6mm. thick and 2.5cm. wide and have an overlap 42cm. long; they are nailed into the shell and not glued and may have been formed directly into the shell. If the drum under construction is more than about 50cm. deep, it may be advisable to fit a third strengthening ring about half-way down. If the rings are to be made separately, rather than directly into the drum, another former will be needed; the outside diameter of the rings must match the inside diameter of the shell and the diameter of the former must be that of the inside diameter of the rings. The rings should be nailed to the shell, using flat-headed nails driven from the outside and hammered well down so that the nail heads do not catch on the skin. For the same reason, when the overlap of the shell is nailed, flat-headed nails should be used at the extremities, with larger, round-headed nails used for the ornamental pattern which starts clear of the heads.

Once the shell is made and the strengthening rings fitted, cut the snare beds diametrically opposite each other. These should be in the batter head end, or both ends, for the tabors, probably in the batter head end for the small, 15cm. side drum, and in the other end only, the modern snare head end, for the larger side drums. The shallow tabor, if it is to have a snare at both ends, should have the beds at one end north and south and at the other east and west; the deeper tabors can either be arranged the same way or have both snares running north and south. The bed must be at least as deep as the snare is thick and about 4cm. wide, sloping gradually up and down again with no sharp corners, to ensure that the snare lies properly and that the skin does not pucker. Smooth the edge of the shell very carefully; any splinters left at this stage will mean torn drum heads later. Rubbing the edges with a block of paraffin wax allows the heads to move more easily. The highest point of the rim of the shell (fig. d), the cut-off point for the head, must be precisely cylindrical; if anything has gone slightly adrift in the forming, it may be possible to correct it while smoothing.

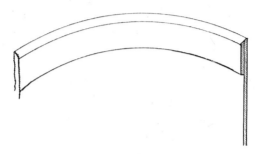

Fig. d
The rim of the shell chamfered down from the outside edge

Next fit the snare strainer. Because the collar of the head comes 2 or 3cm. down the shell, the snare strainers must be at least 8cm. down the shell on the large tabor, though less on the shallower drums for lack of space. The shallowest tabor can have them half-way down the shell. Supporting blocks must be fitted inside the shell to take them, since the shell alone will not be strong enough to bear the strain. If fiddle pegs are used, as suggested on p.24, drill a hole through the shell of the same diameter as the tip of the peg; the snare comes off the side of the peg, not the centre, so the holes must be placed with their edges under the middle of the snare bed. Shape a block to fit the curvature of the shell and fix it over the hole with screws or nails; screws are anachronistic but safer and can be counter-sunk and painted over. Drill through the original hole through the block. Enlarge the hole very slightly with a reamer of the same taper as the peg; not too much, for the peg must fit tightly. If a military snare screw hook is used on the larger side drum, this will be bolted through the block, whose thickness must accommodate the length of the bolt; if it is short, a metal plate about 5cm. square could be used to spread the strain, instead of a block.

[6]

The air hole should now be drilled and should be about 1cm. in diameter. When there was a nail pattern on the overlap, the air hole was traditionally at its centre. Otherwise, the position on the circumference is immaterial, but it is normally placed half-way from head to head and it must not be covered by the player's body. The drum can now be painted or stained or varnished, as the player prefers. If it is to be painted, any nail pattern should be left until the paint is dry; if it is nailed first, the pattern will not show through the paint. The pattern can be marked out with dividers, at least for the central rose, so that the air hole can be drilled; the scratch lines will show through the paint. Dome-headed carpet tacks of the same sort that will be used to secure the head on the timbrel are suitable for the pattern.

One must now decide how the drum is to be suspended. A small side drum can be held by passing a belt through a pair of tension lines, but a permanently fitted strap is more secure. A larger side drum can also be suspended from a belt, but it is better to buy a military drum sling which can be hooked on to a pair of lines or into a ring screwed to the upper counter hoop. A small tabor will need a wrist strap which, again, can either be passed under a couple of tension lines or be fixed to the shell. A larger tabor will need a shoulder strap which must be secured to each end of the shell because it runs at the wrong angle to be held by the tension lines. There is no evidence at all as to the methods used to secure straps on the original instruments; the best answer today is to use metal fittings of the sort that are used to hold the straps on babies' prams (fig. e).

Fig. e
Holder for a suspension strap

These should be screwed through the shell into internal blocks. It is essential to decide exactly how the drum is to hang at this stage; if it is left until the heads are fitted, the drum will have to be taken apart again to fit the straps. Equally, it will be a very laborious business to make any alterations once the heads are on. I find it best to hang the tabors so that my left hand can reach a snare peg while playing. This means that if the snare is taken as running from north to south, the strap is fixed about north-west. The fitting must, of course, be fixed where it will be clear of the collar of the head. The straps should be attached to the metal fittings, as described below (p.25), before fixing the fittings to the drum.

The shell is now ready for the heads.

TIMBREL (TAMBOURINE)

The shell for the timbrel is made in exactly the same way as that for the side drums and tabors, save that being so shallow it does not require a strengthening ring. If the timbrel should be the same diameter as one of the other drums, the same former will serve for both. Slots must be cut in the shell, long enough and wide enough to take the jingles, the commonest number of which in the Middle Ages was five pairs. Double rows are often seen, always side by side, = = = = = , and never as today, — — — — — . This must be borne in mind if converting a pre-existing tambourine; it is normally only possible to use instruments with a single row of slots. The manufacture of the jingles is described below (p.24), but their size, both diameter and total thickness, allowing for any doming, must be determined before cutting the slots, since the jingles must have space to rattle if their sound is not to be stifled. Round-ended slots can be made with an electric drill and a router bit and must be 2 or 3cm. longer than the diameter of the jingles; 1 or 2cm. longer is enough if the slots are square-ended. The slots must be wide enough for the jingles to move their own thickness, including dome, apart. There was no thumb-hole, as there is on the modern tambourine, but there must be a gap between two of the slots wide enough for the player's hand; most medieval timbrels had the slots spaced equidistantly.

The pins which hold the jingles should be not more than a third of the thickness of the wood in diameter, and preferably slightly less. For double slots (= = = = =), make sure that the pins are long enough; they need to be 6 to 12mm. less than the depth of the frame. With an exactly vertical drill, make a hole above the centre of each slot from the edge that is going to carry the skin, of a diameter that will just pass the pin. Stop as soon as the bit comes out into the slot. For double slots, continue through the strip of wood between the slots and stop as soon as the bit appears in the lower slot. With a much thinner drill bit, drill on down into the lower part of the frame to give the pin a starting hole and prevent the wood from splitting. Push the pin into the hole until it just appears in the slot, fit the first jingle, push the pin in a bit further, fit the second jingle and push the pin down until it touches the wood on the other side of the slot. Hammer it home and then, with a punch, hammer it down just below the surface of the wood and plug the hole with wax. If the top of the pin is left flush with the surface, the skin will be cut or will get rust spots on it, or both. The timbrel is now ready for its head.

When converting a modern tambourine, the modern jingles must be removed by cutting their pins with wire cutters and then drawing the stubs out with pliers. The slots must then be enlarged for the new jingles. If the work is done carefully so that the head is not damaged, the pins for the jingles can be inserted from the free side of the frame. It is still important to punch the pins down below the surface, so as to avoid scratching the hand while playing.

NAKERS

The manufacture of naker shells may be too complex for the home craftsman. My first pair were made from copper mixing bowls (Plate 6), which fortunately are easily obtainable from kitchen supply houses, but which have the rim rolled over outwards, the wrong way for a drum; they also have a suspension tag riveted to the side, which must be cut off and the rivet hole securely plugged. A rolled rim is essential, partly for strength and partly to avoid cutting the skin, and a wire inside the roll adds strength. A competent metal beater (spinning is anachronistic, though this may not be important) should be able to make bowls, but they will probably have to be beaten against a former and the cost of making the former may exceed the cost of making the bowls. It may therefore be worth getting together with some colleagues and having a batch made up. Remember that one of each pair of bowls must have an air hole precisely at the apex (see *Early Percussion Instruments* for the reasons for this).

The bowls need not necessarily be of metal. I have a successful pair of stoneware and a very good pair of turned wood, so that if either a potter or a wood-turner is available it may be easier to make the bowls from these materials. Copper has the advantage that it is less likely to break than pottery and less likely to warp or split than wood. The illustrations show that various sizes and shapes were used, from hemispherical to almost conical, with the hemispherical apparently in the majority. I have therefore made mine hemispherical, choosing two sizes quite arbitrarily, for the sake of pitch and tonal variety: one pair 25cm. in diameter, the other 20cm.

Because it is not easy to attach the metal fittings for the suspension straps described above to metal or to pottery, I pass a strap through a pair of tension lines on each drum. It is important to keep the buckle done up at all times; it is only too easy to pick up one end of the strap, or one of the drums, and let the other drum fall off the end of the strap on to the floor.

Some nakers had a snare (e.g. p.2 in *Early Percussion Instruments*). This would require a pair of snare beds, made by filing or hammering down the edge on copper and by filing or scraping on pottery or wood. Holes must be drilled for the tension pegs and, certainly with copper and probably for earthenware or wood, blocks must be fitted behind the holes as for the tabors. I could not face the work that this entails when I made my nakers but I am now using a pair by Paul Williamson, which are better than mine and which have snares. The snares can be removed when not required but, because the peg holes must not be left open, the pegs should be replaced in the holes with the snare running round the outside of the shell. I have found that it is not practicable to remove the snares during a concert and then to replace them for another piece, because the snares take time to settle down. It is therefore essential to have more than one pair of nakers, because in the majority of cases no snares are shown.

2

THE HEADS

In the Middle Ages few illustrations show drums with counter hoops. This means that any tension ropes must, as on many non-European drums, pass through the head just above the flesh hoop. A further complication is that the nakers have a hemispherical shell which reduces its diameter from the rim, unlike the modern timpani which have a cylindrical section before the curved bowl commences, so that a wooden flesh hoop would be left out in the air when it was pulled down the side of the drum. The solution that I have adopted is to stitch the heads to a rope ring so that the flesh hoop, being rope, is flexible and follows the shape of the shell. This is ideal for the nakers and works very well. It is not strictly necessary for the tabors, for which wooden flesh hoops can be used. I have found, though, that without a counter hoop to help clamp the skin to the flesh hoop, the lap is liable to pull out from a wooden flesh hoop and therefore I have used rope flesh hoops on all the early drums save for the timbrels, which are differently constructed, the big side drum, which has counter hoops, and the timpani. Instructions follow both for stitching on rope hoops and for lapping on wooden hoops and each maker must decide which is preferable.

The heads should be thicker than those used for a modern drum of similar size; a thin head tends to 'rattle' on a small drum, especially when it is struck with a heavy beater. The best are first-grade, heavy-duty timpani heads or tenor drum heads, but these latter will not be first grade. It is getting more and more difficult to find drum shops that stock calf heads and one of the few reliable manufacturers left is Messrs. H. Band of Brentford, Middlesex. For any drum, the skin must be as wide as the diameter of the drum plus about 18cm. The extra 18cm. is to provide a collar down the side of the shell and to allow enough to stitch or lap to the flesh hoop. For a shallow tabor, an extra 10cm. may be enough, but an excess can always be trimmed off whereas one cannot add anything if one has underestimated.

Skins must always be worked wet so that they are flexible while being worked, and dry taut. The books usually advise soaking for ten minutes; I find half an hour is better. Always use cold water, even in winter; hot water will shrink and shrivel the skin. The bath is the best place to soak the skin; run the water deep enough for the skin to remain submerged as it unrolls. If an old timpani skin is used, which can be a very economical way of getting heads, for many a timpanist throws away a skin that is torn only at the edge, scrub the head well on both surfaces with a good quality toilet soap and a soft nail brush. Soap not only cleans the skin but also renders it more supple and restores the life which has dried out of it. If the head is to be lapped on a wooden hoop, rinse the soap out again or the lap will slip out, but if the head is to be stitched or tacked, as with the timbrel, leave it soapy and rub the soap well into it.

While the skin is soaking, prepare the working area and equipment. A sheet of plate glass is the ideal working surface for lapping; if that is not available, any clean, smooth surface which will not be damaged by wetness and which is large enough to lay the skin down flat on will do. For the other techniques, the surface need not be perfectly smooth but it must be clean and large enough for the skin and able to withstand damp. Newspaper should be avoided as a protective covering since the print comes off and will be transferred to the skin. Either buy a proper lapping tool from a drum shop or use a dessert spoon with a smoothly bent-up end; check that the edges of either are smooth and will not damage the skin. Some wooden or plastic spring clothes pegs are useful when lapping; not metal pegs, which may leave rust marks. An indelible or copying pencil which will mark on wet vellum will be needed to mark the head, and a spacing block: a piece of wood with one or more holes of a diameter to take the pencil drilled in it 2 or 3cm. from the end. For the timbrel, a hammer will be needed, some cord, some dome-headed tacks such as large carpet tacks, and a very sharp knife or razor blade with which to trim the head. For stitching, a needle and stout thread are necessary; a synthetic thread such as the thinner terylene whipping twine, which can be bought from yacht chandlers, is best so that there is no trouble with shrinkage if the skin needs to be resoaked. A pair of strong scissors or tin snips will be needed to trim the skin, for this is never supplied cut exactly to size. The ropes and buffs of the tension cords must be ready before one starts on the skin; these are described below on p.27. The flesh hoops must also be ready.

A wooden flesh hoop is made in the same way as the strengthening hoops inside the drum shell. It must be of such a diameter that it fits the outside of the shell with sufficient clearance for two thicknesses of the tension rope. For the later drums which have counter hoops, less clearance is necessary and 2mm. should suffice. Modern drums have square section wooden flesh hoops, about 1cm. wide and thick, but the older drums usually had rectangular section hoops made of a wooden strip perhaps 12mm. wide by 5 or 6mm. thick. A flesh hoop usually has an overlap 10 to 15cm. long cut as a long scarfe joint. A common material today is beech.

A rope flesh hoop should be spliced, using pre-stretched terylene, the same rope as will be suggested for the tension ropes, so that it will not be affected by the wet head; a rope of natural fibre would shrink if the head had to be resoaked. A short splice will suffice, if the ends are tapered, but it will make the hoop thicker at that point; a long splice is much better. Books on knots and splices can also be obtained at yacht chandlers, along with the terylene twine and rope. When splicing terylene, at least one more tuck in each direction is necessary than the books suggest for natural rope, because there is less friction with synthetic fibres than with natural ones. Splicing is necessary because any knot would make a lump. A rope of about 4mm. diameter will be suitable for the nakers, the small tabor, and side drum; 7mm. is better for the large tabor. The large side drum and the long drum, being later in date and having counter hoops, should have their heads lapped on wooden hoops. The rope hoop, being flexible, should be an exact fit to the rim of the drum. If, when it is finished, it is on the tight side, the lapping tool can be used like a tyre lever to help it on to the shell.

TIMBREL

The timbrel has no flesh hoop; the skin is nailed directly to the frame. Holes should be drilled in the frame, about 1cm. from the edge from which the pins that hold the jingles were driven, 2 or 3cm. apart in an even line to receive the nails. The jingles must already have been fitted; check that their pins are all below the surface of the frame. Lay the skin on the working surface, the smoother side of the skin downwards. Every skin has a face and a back; one plays on the face, the smoother side (the modern tambourine player prefers to play on the back, the roughness of which helps the thumb roll). Place the timbrel on the skin, the edge with the row of holes downwards. Allow 6 or 7cm. of skin to project all round the timbrel. Fold the skin up against the outside of the timbrel and tie a cord tightly round it just below the jingles. Pull the skin taut through the cord and push one of the nails through it and into one of the holes drilled for it. Do the same on the opposite side of the timbrel, making sure that while the head is taut, it is not so tight that any strain folds or creases have formed and that the instrument has not been pulled into an oval instead of a circle. Calling these points north and south, do the same east and west, followed by north-east, south-west, north-west, and south-east; always work from opposite points. Now fill the gaps between these points, trying to niggle at the head so that each nail is placed without any folds appearing in the skin. In theory, of course, this is impossible; one cannot fold a flat skin over the edge of a circle without folds appearing. In practice, it can be done, or nearly done, by pulling slightly here and making a slight adjustment there. Folds on the side of the timbrel are unsightly and folds projecting over the rim into the playing area make for poor tone. When all the nails are set, hammer the points over inside the shell; go carefully because if the hammer hits the skin it will tear it and the job will have to be done again from the beginning. See that the points are flat against the shell so that they cannot catch a finger. Trim off the surplus skin, keeping as straight a line as possible, for the sake of appearance, and leaving just enough for the domed heads of the nails to be in the centre of the skin on the side of the frame. Leave the timbrel, well away from any source of heat and out of the light of the sun, for twenty-four hours before playing it.

The trimmings from the skin can be used to tie the buffs (p.28) for the tabors and nakers.

LAPPING

To lap on a wooden flesh hoop, lay the skin down, smooth side downwards, place the drum shell on the skin, and, with the indelible pencil in the appropriate hole of the spacing block, draw a circle round the drum at the same distance from the drum as the depth of the collar desired. There must be a collar, for if there were not, the head would sit on the top of the drum; the hoop must come a little way down the side of the drum and this distance is called the collar. The small side drum and shallow tabor need at least 15mm., the medium tabor and the nakers about 25mm., and the large tabor about 4cm. Remove the drum shell and lay the flesh hoop on the skin. The pencil circle, which will be outside the flesh hoop, must be drawn to it by placing inverted saucers or soup plates under the centre of the skin until the two meet each other. With the scissors or tin snips, trim the skin so that enough projects beyond the flesh hoop to completely enfold the hoop plus the depth of the hoop again (see fig. f). It is safest to draw a circle at the correct distance beyond the first circle before cutting; for a hoop 12mm. wide by 6mm. thick, the circle must be 5cm. beyond the first circle: 12mm. twice and 6mm. twice plus another 12mm. Fold this extra skin over the hoop and, with the lapping tool or spoon handle, push the surplus up between the hoop and the skin as in fig. f. Do the same at the opposite point on the hoop, being careful not to pull so tight that the other side of the hoop comes up into the air; keep it flat on the table. If the first tuck starts to unlap itself, put a clothes peg on it to hold it. Lap north, south, east, west, north-east, south-west, north-west, south-east. Then fill the gaps between these points, again niggling the skin so as to avoid unsightly folds. Not all folds can be avoided, but keep them as small as possible and make sure that they do not project onto the playing area. Leave any clothes pegs in position for an hour or so.

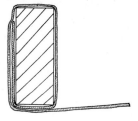

Fig. f
The head lapped on a wooden flesh hoop

When both heads are lapped and the second head has had half an hour to an hour to set, rub powdered french chalk (or talcum powder) inside the hoops so that they do not stick to the drum shell as the skin dries, and mount the heads on the drum. Both the heads must be lapped within the same period; if this is not possible, the first head must be placed on the drum, after it has had time to set, so that it does not twist the flesh hoop as it dries; some distortion is almost inevitable unless the whole job can be done in one session. The head would then have to be taken off the drum when the second head is ready and resoaked for two or three minutes and repowdered; if the resoaking allows the lap to come out at any point, all traces of powder must be removed and the lap tucked back before re-powdering. Rope up the drum as described below on p.18 and leave it away from heat and sun for twenty-four hours to dry. The roping is then finished off, the snare fitted, and the drum is ready to play.

STITCHING

Stitching a head requires the minimum of skill and the maximum of patience. When the job is done, the head will look like a shallow circular tray with vertical sides, like the lid of a round biscuit tin. To achieve this, a pencilled circle of, for example, 30cm. diameter must be persuaded to go on to a 25cm. diameter rope ring. In order to avoid folds and an uneven head, the skin must be pursed up evenly on the rope and this cannot be done if one tries to do the whole circumference by eye. It can, however, be done an eighth at a time.

Lay the skin down, smooth side downwards, and draw the circle for the collar round the drum shell with the pencil and spacing block. Mark on this circle north, south, east, west, north-east, south-west, north-west, south-east. Mark the same points on the rope ring, making sure that all the marks are accurately placed; if any are not, the head will be uneven and the tone poor. Stitch the skin to the rope at each of these points, north to north, south to south, and so on, with a single stitch at each point, passing through the skin and the rope and the skin again and knotted off. With a long thread, stitch round the head, turning the surplus skin inside over the rope and passing the thread over the rope and through both thicknesses of the skin, as in fig. g. The stitches should be at least 3mm. apart (if they are closer the skin may tear) but not more than 6mm. apart or they will not grip properly. Every fifth or sixth stitch should pass through the rope to hold everything together. One can see how much surplus skin must be pursed up on to the rope in each eighth of the circumference; try to pull up the same amount at each stitch so that it is even all the way round. If possible, stitch the whole head with one long thread; otherwise, knot a new length on to the old with a surgeon's knot, a reef knot with an extra turn in each half (a normal reef will not grip with a synthetic thread).

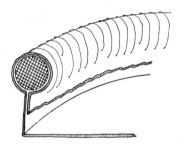

Fig. g
The head stitched on a rope flesh hoop

When the job is finished, trim off any excess fringe inside the head, not cutting too close to the stitches, for the holes for the tension ropes should pass through both thicknesses of skin, but close enough for none of the fringe to be left inside the rim of the drum. Powder the inside of the head, as with the lapped head, and fit it on the drum. If it is too tight to get it on, soak it for two or three minutes to relax it, repowder it, and try again. On the tabors and small side drum, the other head must be made before the first one has had time to dry out so much that it would be dangerous to start roping it. The nakers have only one head and can now be roped up.

The rope and the buffs should be ready (see p.27). Holes can be punched in the head for the rope, or they can be burned in with a red-hot iron, but be careful because heat will melt synthetic thread and burn natural thread. A burnt hole has the advantage that a hard ring is formed round the edge. The easiest method is to use a larding needle, a needle used for threading strips of fat through lean meat, which has a hollow end into which the end of the rope can be pushed, so that the holes can be made and the rope drawn through them at the same time. Do not use the larding needles with an eye in the end like a giant sewing needle; they would make too large a hole. The holes should be as close to the flesh hoop as possible or they will be torn larger as the tension pulls the rope down to the hoop, but not so close that they cut the threads on the stitched hoops.

Since the nakers have only one head, I use an iron ring 2 or 3cm. in diameter to hold the other end of the tension lines. Mark the head equidistantly and accurately (using a tape measure and not guess-work) for the number of tension lines to be used. With the tabors and side drum, mark the other head so that its holes will come exactly half-way between those of the first head. Starting at one of these marks on the non-batter head (but on the batter head for the nakers), put the rope through from above, so that the rope goes through the head and then between the head and the shell, and pull it right through so that the eye splice at the far end of the rope is against the head, as in fig. h. Pass the rope through a buff and down to the equivalent mark on the batter head (or to the iron ring on the nakers). Again pass it through from the outside, through the head (or over the ring) and down between the head and the shell (or between the ring and the shell) and then pass it again through the same

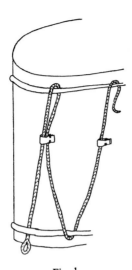

Fig. h

Roping up a tabor or side drum; the arrowheads point in the direction in which
the rope is moving

buff. Go back to the next mark on the first head and do the same again.
For the sake of neatness, make sure that all the buffs are the same way
round; the buffs have a knot side and a plain side and the drum looks
better if, with the buffs all turned in one direction, all the knots are out-
wards or inwards rather than haphazard. Do not try to pull the rope tight
at this stage; keep the ring roughly central on the apex of the nakers and
try to keep the rope from twisting as it is pulled through, but leave it a
little slack. If, with a shallow tabor, buffs are wanted at both ends of each
tension line, after pulling the eye splice to the head, put two buffs on the
rope, one facing each way, then pass through the batter head and through
the buff nearer the batter head (not through the buff nearer the eye splice;
that will be for the tail of the rope on the final V), add another buff and
through the first head again, through the new buff and add another one,
and so on. When the rope has gone right round the drum, knot its tail
through the eye. The drum should now have the rope going up and down
in narrow Vs, all of them a little loose and sloppy. Standing the drum

with the batter head downwards, every V should have a buff round the two ropes at its point; a drum with double buffs will have a buff round the point of each V and of each Λ; the nakers will have buffs round the point of each Λ. Put the drum away from heat and sun for twenty-four hours, with neither head touching anything: on its side across the corner of a table in a cool, shady room, for instance.

Working very gently, tighten the rope, starting from the first line, i.e., pulling the eye splice to the head. Pull the next strand tight, but not too tight; if this first round leaves the rope too loose, one can always go round again, as will be necessary after the drum has been used for a little while. Then tighten the next strand and so on all round the drum, being very careful that the heads are not pulled lop-sided on the drum and that the iron ring stays centrally on the apex of the bowl of the nakers. A repetition of rounds, little by little, is much better than pulling a head lop-sided or tearing it. When the ropes are tight enough, not for playing, which comes next, but for storage, knot off with a couple of half hitches through the eye. Coil the tail of spare rope out of the way for the moment. Pull the buffs down, always working by opposites, north and south, east and west, and so on, and see what the drum sounds like. If the heads seem too slack, pull the buffs down further. The rope may need to be tightened again; it will certainly need to be tightened after playing a few times, for even a pre-stretched rope will stretch a little. To do so, slacken the buff on the V with the eye splice and pull up the slack, probably only gaining 1cm. or so on each V, always going away from the splice towards the tail of the rope, and so on round the drum, slackening each V in turn, but still making sure that the heads are not pulled lop-sided. On all other occasions the Vs must be slackened, as they are tightened, by opposites. When the circuit is finished, re-knot the tail of the rope through the eye. Finally, make one last tightening by threading the tail of the rope through the points of the Vs as in fig. i and then pulling the tail tight so that it makes a straight line and each V becomes a looped V as in fig. j. When the tail has come round to the eye again, knot it through the eye and use up any spare rope in the traditional drummer's plait, or chain knot as most books on knots and splices call it, catching into the plait any Vs that it passes.

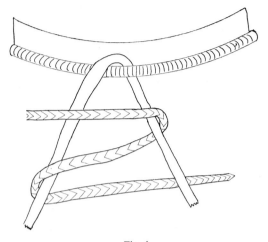

Fig. i
Passing the tail of the rope through the Vs; the arrowheads point in the direction
of travel

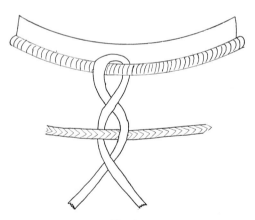

Fig. j
Pulling the tail of the rope straight after it has passed through the Vs.

There are two main advantages in the use of counter hoops on the
large side drum and the other later drums: one is that the heads need not
be pierced for the tension lines; the other that the drum can be played on

a stand without affecting the tone greatly, although it will look as ana-chronistic as a viol with a tail-spike. The counter hoop must be exactly the same diameter as the flesh hoop and the same thickness, but deeper, i.e., made of a wider piece of wood. It must be rounded on the edge away from the head, so as not to fray the tension ropes, and flat on the other edge so as to grip on the flesh hoop and the head. It is usually painted or stained to match or to contrast with the shell. Holes are bored from side to side, one for each tension point, either horizontally through the wood or on a slight diagonal so that the opening on the outside of the hoop is slightly nearer the shell than that on the inside. The counter hoop on the snare head (on the later side drums the lower head) must have channels cut so that the snare can run freely between the counter hoop and the flesh hoop. To avoid a conflict, make these channels half-way between two rope holes. Set the hoop for the snare head in position, with the channels over the centre of the snare beds, and then set the hoop on the batter head so that its holes come exactly half-way between those of the snare hoop. Rope up as above, starting from the snare head end, passing the rope always over the hoop and down through the holes from the inside of the hoop to the outside. As with the tabors, the buffs should all be on the points of the Vs nearest to the batter head. Tighten up and finish off exactly as above.

3

THE FITTINGS

The snare is a strand of gut of a weight appropriate to the size of the drum and the thickness of the heads. Because both of these vary from drum to drum, some experiment will be necessary. As a rough guide, a snare about twice as heavy as one would think suitable for a modern drum of the same size would be best to start with. A gut snare from a normal military drum is about right for the nakers or small side drum or the smallest tabor. Soft gut is better than hard, and oiled gut, such as is used for clock weights, works well on the large tabor. For the big side drum, one needs something altogether heavier; on my 56cm. diameter drum, I use a double strand of a very thick, plain gut double bass string, 5mm. in diameter.

The tabors, and the nakers when they were snared, always had a single snare but, certainly by Praetorius's time and probably earlier, the side drum had either two or four strands, and by Handel's time four or six. It was always an even number because the snare is either one long strand, going back and forth across the head, or a number of double strands. English eighteenth-century side drums did not usually have a snare strainer. There was no snare channel cut in the counter hoop and the snare was simply held between the counter and the flesh hoops, a knot at each end preventing it from slipping out. This works, but only moderately well, since there is no way of adjusting the snare tension and the response will therefore vary according to the humidity of the air. Because screw tensioning for the snare can be seen in Praetorius's illustration, I bought and fitted a modern, old-fashioned military drum screw hook and block for the big side drum. A modern orchestral drum snare strainer with quick release would look wrong and would probably not be strong enough for so heavy a snare, but the only difference between the old-fashioned military screw and that shown by Praetorius is the shape of the wing nut which controls the tension.

There is no evidence whether or how the snare tension was controlled on the early tabors and nakers. As stated above, I have followed the modern Basque practice of using a fiddle peg, using a size of peg that suits the appearance of the drum, violin for the small ones and viola for the larger. One can either use a peg on each end of the snare or a peg on one end and a simple knob screwed through the drum shell into a block for the other. There is a slight advantage in being able to adjust the tension from either end. The hole in the shank of the peg must be drilled or reamered out, since the snare will be thicker than the violin or viola string for which it was designed. The snare must be long enough to take three or four turns round the peg at each end, to give a secure grip. If a knob is used on one end, the snare must be knotted round it. Gut knots quite easily if it is soaked for a few minutes, either standing the part that is to be knotted in a glass of water or holding it in the mouth. When a single snare is used, its tension is critical for the tone of the drum and must be adjusted every time the drum is played as carefully as a string player adjusts the strings of a viol or rebec when tuning.

TIMBREL JINGLES

Discs for timbrel jingles can be cut from sheet brass, stamped out from sheet, or cast by a brass-founder. The thickness and the hardness of the jingles control their tone: the thicker and softer the more bell-like, the thinner and harder the more rattling they will sound. There is no conclusive evidence as to what sort of jingles were originally used; some illustrations appear to show thin ones and some clearly show thick, cast jingles; the best answer for the conscientious player will be to have several timbrels, each with a different type of jingle, in order to have a choice of sonorities. The alternative is to choose one that one likes the sound of and stick to it.

I use jingles cut from sheet brass about 0.75mm. in thickness and about 7cm. in diameter. They are marked out in the sheet with a pair of dividers and the pin-hole drilled in the centre of each disc before they are cut out.

The discs are then hammered with a very heavy hammer on a lead block, which domes them and hardens them. The pin hole, which should be between one and half times and twice the diameter of the pin, so that the jingles are held only loosely, is distorted by the hammering but can be easily cleaned out; it would be difficult to drill it once the jingles were shaped.

A colleague stamps his jingles from the same gauge of brass and, because the stamping machine leaves them slightly domed, does not hammer them. This makes a considerable difference to the tone: mine produce a sort of rustling clatter, while his produce a bell-like ring. The shape is different: mine are domed like miniature cymbals and his are smoothly curved right across the disc; mine, of course, are slightly thinner after being hammered. He has recently taken to hammering his, producing a more clattering sound which we both prefer; each maker, however, must decide which sound is the best.

As far as one can tell from the pictures, cast jingles should not be more than about 2.5mm. in thickness after they have been turned on a lathe to remove the pits left by sand-casting. The diameters of early jingles varied from about 4cm. to about 10cm. Bear in mind that the larger the jingles, the larger the timbrel must be to accommodate them and the heavier and the more tiring it will be to play.

SUSPENSION STRAPS

Leather straps about 3cm. in width, such as luggage straps or stirrup leathers, with buckles so that they can be adjusted for length, are the most comfortable. Some of the instruments are heavy enough to make it worth thinking of one's comfort and not economising or taking short cuts at this point. For the sake of the appearance of the instruments, it is worth making a proper craftsman's job of attaching the straps.

For a small side drum or a wrist tabor, take a length of good quality leather strap, sufficient to go round the waist or wrist respectively. If it is just too wide for the metal fitting (see fig. e on p.7), it can be reduced by cutting an arc out of each side of the strap at the point at which it will be fixed. Cut the strap to length, with enough to go through the buckle and to spare; in performance, the drum may be worn over evening dress or period costume and, if more than one member of the ensemble plays percussion, one must allow for a change of girth as well as a change of costume. Take about 7cm. of the cut-off portion, or of another identical strap, and lay this over the strap, inside of the leather to inside, with the metal fitting centrally between them and stitch the one to the other as in fig. k. One could rivet them together, but stitching looks better and is stronger. Handicraft shops sell multi-pointed starred wheels which will mark the leather in evenly spaced holes and at least start to pierce the holes for the stitches. Take a long thread with a needle at each end of it and pass each needle through the same hole in the opposite direction; in this way one has continuous stitches on each side of the strap, instead of - - - - -. Waxed cobbler's thread is the best, with cobbler's or bookbinder's needles; the triangular needles sometimes sold for leather work, although better at piercing the leather, often cut the other thread. One or two sail-maker's palms with which to push the needles through are essential; one can buy them both left and right handed at the same yacht chandlers as the terylene twine and rope and the book on knots and splices which will also be needed. Ordinary dressmaker's thimbles are too thin and are easily pierced when stitching leather.

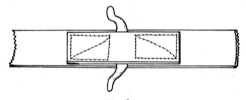

Fig. k
Stitching the suspension strap for the small tabor or side drum

A shoulder strap needs to be stitched differently, since the two ends are attached to opposite ends of the drum. The buckle end should be on a short length of strap; bend the end of the strap over the fitting, inside to inside, and stitch it to itself. Then do the same with the tail of the strap, allowing enough length to go over the shoulder and into the buckle, holding the drum at the most comfortable height for playing (this can be established by getting somebody else to hold the drum at various heights). Fix the buckle to the lower end of the drum, behind the player's back, and the tail to the upper end; there is then no risk of the buckle coming on to the shoulder. Check before starting to stitch that the buckle is going to be the right way round and that the inside of the leather is going to be towards the drum. With the wrist strap and the belt strap, on the other hand, the outside of the leather will be towards the drum. In all cases, the inside of the leather will be towards the player's body, as a belt normally is. Finally, punch holes to fit the pin of the buckle 2 or 3cm. apart in the tail of the strap, continuing far enough to allow for any variation of dress or player, and screw the fittings to the drum.

TENSION ROPES AND BUFFS

For the tension cord, I use a modern synthetic rope, pre-stretched terylene, 4mm. in diameter for the tabors, nakers, and small side drum, and 7mm. for the big side drum. This avoids the shrinking and stretching that accompany changes of humidity with ropes of natural fibre, and also avoids the excessive stretching of nylon or untreated terylene. This can be bought at yacht chandlers or good rope shops. It is a fairly soft rope, which is an advantage when leading it round the drum, but it has the normal disadvantages of the synthetic in that it is smooth, so that splices must be made with more tucks than usual, and that the end frays when being worked; it can be secured either by putting adhesive tape round the end or by searing it in a flame.

One needs at least twelve to sixteen pairs of tensioning lines, or Vs, for any drum, depending upon its diameter; a number divisible by four makes marking the head out much easier. The length of cord for a drum can be found by multiplying twice the number of tension lines by the depth of the drum and adding two circumferences, plus a metre or two to be on the safe side. For the nakers, the addition of one circumference plus a bit for safety will probably be enough, since the lower end of the tension lines will be held by a small ring. I find that sixteen or twenty lines are best for 25cm. nakers and twelve or sixteen for 20cm.; the closer together the lines are, the less strain there is on any point of the head. An eye splice in the end of the rope looks much better, and is much more secure, than a knot. The eye should be kept quite small; about twice the diameter of the rope is enough.

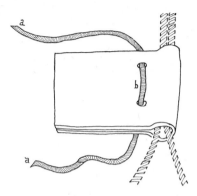

Fig. 1

Tying the buffs. Tie the ends (a) so that the knot lies above the loop (b).
The dotted lines show how the tension ropes will run when the buff is
placed on the drum

Each tension line must have a leather buff; a shallow drum may be
more efficiently tensioned from both ends and will then need two buffs
to each line. In the early periods, the lines seem to have been tightened
by thongs tied round them and such thongs, made of strong leather boot-
laces or similar material, can be used instead of buffs if preferred. They
should be tied as tightly as possible round the batter head point of each **V**.
Buffs are made by folding and tying short pieces of leather strap and their
size should correspond to that of the drum; too large or too small look
silly, so try various sizes against the shell to see what will look best. It
will be easier to fold the straps tightly if they are first soaked in neat's-foot
oil. The buffs must be tied as closely to the fold as possible, allowing just
enough room for two thicknesses of tension rope, and they must be wide
enough to have two holes for their tie punched across the width of the
strap; one hole will not allow the buff to be gripped sufficiently firmly.
Tie the buffs with soaking wet strips of spare drum head, so that the ties
grip very tightly as they dry. Pass the strips through the holes as in fig. 1,
bringing the ends up round the sides, pulling tight and tying in a reef
knot above the space between the two holes; if the knot shows a tendency
to slip, take an extra turn in each half, as in a surgeon's knot.

4

THE BEATERS

The pictures of early drummers show that the beaters were thick and clumsy, like miniature clubs. Everything about a beater affects the tone that it produces: the weight, the thickness, both at the point where it touches the drum head and elsewhere along its length, the hardness, and the length, so that considerable experiment may be necessary in order to design the most effective beater for each drum. Beaters should be made of a fairly dense hardwood which will turn well on the lathe, leaving a smooth surface, and which will not splinter or chip in use. Hickory is good; box is excellent as are most of the fruit woods of similar sort, the woods that were used for 'boxwood' woodwind instruments; mahogany is worth trying, although it was not known at this period (old furniture is a source of well-seasoned timber); rosewood, also anachronistic, is good but some people are allergic to it; beech is tolerable as a makeshift. For those who have no lathe, nor access to a wood turner, the heavy hickory modern marching bass drum beaters are, although on the large side, excellent for the larger tabors and may work on the smaller drums also; they suit my own nakers but not Paul Williamson's pair, for which the beaters he makes of beech are better.

Any piece of wood will, like a xylophone bar, produce a note of definite pitch and if the two pitches of a pair of beaters are not the same, one cannot produce the same sound from each hand. This does not affect the tabor, where only one hand is used, but it is very important on the nakers and the side drums. If a certain pair of sticks are ideal, save for a pitch difference, they can be tuned: thinning the centre, measured from one end to the other, will flatten the pitch; thinning either or both ends will sharpen it. Go very carefully; a very slight difference in thickness makes quite a difference to the pitch. One is not aiming at a perfect unison, but only at something less than a quarter tone apart. When buying sticks, go to a shop that caters for the professional drummer and try a handful of sticks and match up the pairs; they will be accustomed to the vagaries of their customers.

Too heavy a stick kills the tone of the drum, whereas too light a stick seems only to tap the surface and does not draw out the full tone. The only recourse for those who have never played a drum before, and who do not know what sort of tone the drum is capable of producing, is to obtain a range of sticks of different weights and, over a period of time, decide which is best or at which end of the range more beaters must be sought, heavier or lighter. As a rough guide, choose heavier rather than lighter; most of these drums respond best to a heavy stick and one can play lightly with a heavy beater, but one cannot make a light beater give more than its weight allows.

Beaters for the Dürer size side drum were quite small, with a cylindrical stick and a spherical bead. Any of the heavier woods mentioned above might be suitable, as would ebony which is excellent for side drum sticks, though too heavy for the club like tabor and naker beaters. The sticks for the larger side drums were similar in shape to the modern side drum sticks but considerably thicker and with much heavier beads. The specialist military band drum dealers often have very large and very heavy ebony side drum sticks and these may be heavy enough for a 56cm. or a Handelian side drum. A full size 75-80cm. side drum will require something heavier still because the weight of the stick must relate to the size of the drum, however tiring it may be for the player's wrists.

The heads of timpani sticks were sometimes round, either spherical or ovoid, and sometimes discs. The common materials seem to have been wood or ivory, but discs may also have been made of hard leather; three thicknesses of the leather used for shoe heels glued together and then shaped to a disc with rounded edges makes an effective head. The ovoids of lignum vitae which plumbers use as bobs on lead piping also make effective heads; they can be found in various sizes and each size will produce a different tone quality. These heads can be fitted to shafts of whatever material suits the player. Cane, such as is often used today, should be avoided since there is no evidence for flexible shafts before the nineteenth century. I use 9mm. aluminium tubing, also anachronistic, but it is what I use for my modern timpani sticks and it seems to work well on the early ones. I use heads of various sizes, shapes, and materials on shafts 35cm. long, a length that I find comfortable. On the double drums, which are extra large eighteenth-century timpani (mine measure 68.5 and 84cm. in diameter and 44.5cm. in depth; the pair which Handel used to borrow from the Tower seem to have been slightly larger, though probably no deeper), I use a pair of wooden marching bass drum beaters (See Plate 1, 1 and Plate 4). These are a little larger than any surviving eighteenth-century beaters that I have seen, but so are the timpani. Some of the surviving timpani beaters are much the same shape as these, quite thick with a large ovoid head. Others have disc-shaped heads around 4cm. in diameter and quite slender shafts 22-25cm. long of either wood or ivory, sometimes with the head turned with the shaft, sometimes with an added head. The integral head is stronger but also much more expensive since it means starting with a much thicker billet of wood or ivory. Hickory is probably the best wood to use today for shafts; lancewood may make a tolerable substitute: greenheart, such as is used for fishing rods, may be worth trying. Other woods used historically include boxwood and servicewood.

The beaters for the xylophone seem, in the very indistinct illustrations, to have been either discs or cylinders, or perhaps spheres, of wood on wooden shafts. These must be held very lightly if they are to produce a good tone. Today, shafts are usually of cane, which will produce a different sound, and only a very few makers provide wooden heads. One can sometimes pick up old pairs with boxwood heads but these will almost certainly be on malacca cane shafts. Any plastics and rubbers should be avoided; their different weights and hardness will falsify the sound.

Beaters for the dulcimer and for the long drum have been described in *Early Percussion Instruments*, but briefly, a light wooden beater, such as an unpadded cimbalom beater, is best for the dulcimer. Some boxwood tools for carving clay look exactly like renaissance dulcimer beaters and may be worth trying. The long drum is struck on one head with a wooden beater, such as the marching bass drum beater already referred to, and on the other with a switch (Plate 1, 2), traditionally of birch twigs like a miniature gardener's besom, which can be made up from basketwork cane.

The beater for the tambourin de Béarn is a cylindrical rod, about 2cm. in thickness, sometimes swelling to a handle at one end. Boxwood has been used. The cylindrical shape is important since all the strings must be struck simultaneously. I have made mine by cutting the contracting portion off the end of an old, heavy side drum stick, leaving a beater 34.5cm. long.

The triangle beater is normally made of the same metal and the same thickness as the triangle, though, provided that the difference is not too great, there is no harm if it is a little thinner or thicker. The end of the beater may be turned in a ring, to make it easier to hold, by heating and bending it. The modern beater, usually a six-inch nail, is too light and too soft; a carriage bolt is better than a nail, though still on the soft side. Steel can be hardened by tempering it.

5

MISCELLANEOUS

Only pellet bells of cast brass are worth using. Those usually sold today as drummers' sleigh bells or for children's toys are stamped sheet metal and quite useless for any serious purpose. Old sets of proper drummers' bells can sometimes be found in shops that deal in secondhand instruments, and they and harness bells can occasionally be bought in antique shops or in horse harness shops. Cast pellet bells can still be bought new in France, where they are used as small sheep bells, and in America from some of the supply houses which cater to the American Indian dancer.

When pellet bells are attached to a timbrel, either as well as or instead of jingles, they can be mounted either in circular holes in the frame, large enough for them to swing without knocking on the wood, or in small holes just big enough to take the tang of the bell, in both cases mounted on pins of the same sort as are used to hold the jingles. A third method is to drill two small holes through the frame and to pass a soft wire through the holes and through the tang of the bell, twisting or knotting the ends of the wire together inside the frame. Too many pellet bells on a timbrel will make it very heavy and tiring to play.

Pellet bells on a wrist strap can be made either by finding ready-made wrist-support straps strong enough to take half a dozen bells or by cutting down lengths of leather strap, similar to that used to suspend the drums, but at least 4cm. wide. (Plate 8.) The latter may be preferable, since when one is playing in formal dress, the straps must go outside the coat sleeves and a wrist-support strap may not be long enough. Stitch or wire six bells of 2.5 or 4cm. diameter to the strap, three along each edge. Wiring is stronger but to avoid tearing the clothes or scratching the wrist, knot or twist the wire on the outer surface of the strap, not the inner.

A very effective, although quite artificial, instrument can be made by fixing a number of bells on to a wooden bar. Take 75cm. or so of 5 by 5cm. timber, and round and smooth 10 to 15cm. at each end as a handle. Thread a length of wire such as 2mm. galvanised wire through the hole in the tangs of a dozen or so bells, looping it round each tang. Attach the wire to the wood with a fencing staple at each end and between each bell. Repeat on each face of the wood and the result will be a very heavy and very loud instrument. I seldom use the one that I have made and it has not really justified its cost, for the bells are not cheap, simply because it is too loud. On the other hand, just occasionally it has been very useful, particularly out of doors.

TRIANGLE

I have not yet succeeded in making a triangle which looks like those in the illustrations of the period and which produces a tolerable sound. The pictures almost all show a closed frame, in the shape of a triangle or trapezium, carrying rings on the lower horizontal bar. All those that I have made, or have had made by other people, with a closed frame, produce a dull clank which is quite unacceptable. Using an open frame, with the opening upwards so that the rings do not fall out of the gap, I have produced a triangle with an excellent sound (Plate 9); a colleague has produced an instrument, also with a good sound, making the frame with so small a gap that the triangle can be held in the normal position without the rings escaping. It must be borne in mind, however, that these triangles are not, so far as we know, authentic.

Both the triangle and its rings should be made of steel, the rings somewhat lighter than the triangle. One could buy a commercial triangle and buy, or make, steel rings for it, or make one's own. Some people maintain that silver steel, a form of tool steel easily obtainable in short lengths, is close in character to medieval steel; others, who may be more reliable, say that it is not. The standard length of silver steel bars is 33cm. which will produce a small, though adequate, triangle. The steel rod has to be bent into shape. With only a gas cooker in which to heat it, 6.5mm. steel is about as thick as can be bent; with a bunsen burner or a good blow lamp, 9cm. or a bit over should be possible. A vice, a pair of heavy

[34]

pliers, a file, and a large bowl or bucket of cold water will be needed.

Mark the steel rod with the file at one third and at two thirds of its length. Hold one of these marks in the flame until the metal glows bright orange, holding it with the pliers, not with the fingers; a pair of heavy leather gloves are an additional protection. Put the rod quickly into the vice, the red hot area just above the jaws, and bend it to 60°. Plunge it into the water and move it around in the water to cool it. Then do the same at the other file mark. The tone of the triangle will depend upon its temper and it should be reheated to whatever stage is preferred and then quenched again. The gas cooker is better than the bunsen burner for tempering, since one can get the whole triangle into the flame. The rings are similarly made, bent into a circle between two pairs of pliers or bent round a mandrel, a rod of suitable diameter. I find that four rings made from 10cm. lengths of 5mm. steel are as much as a triangle made from a 33cm. rod of 6.5mm. steel can carry, and that for quiet playing it is better to take off one or two of the rings.

If the angles of the triangle are made accurately, the gap between the arms will be so small that the rings cannot escape. The rings are placed on the triangle by gently pulling the arms open; they will spring back into place. Tie a loop of nylon or gut just large enough to accommodate the thumb and the triangle; it should be as short as possible to prevent the triangle from swinging around. The modern drummer's triangle clip is a useful gadget, since the triangle can be clipped to the music stand when not in use; never play it while clipped to the stand, for this alters the tone. The clip, made from a bulldog paper clip, as in fig. m, is an invention that all drummers owe to James Blades. Drill two holes in one of the handles and tie a nylon loop just larger than the thickness of the triangle, so that it does not touch the metal of the clip, through the holes. When playing, hold the clip, being careful to keep it level so that it does not touch the triangle. If the gap between the arms of the triangle is too wide to retain the rings, as mine is, drill a small hole through the end of each arm and tie a loop through the holes, suspending the triangle upside down. Alternatively, reheat and rebend the triangle and then temper it again. If the angles are so inaccurate that one arm is longer than the other, saw off a bit until they are equal.

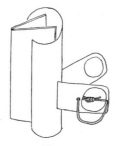

Fig. m
Bulldog clip fitted with a nylon loop to hold the triangle

TONG CYMBALS

Buy two pairs of fireside tongs from an antique or junk shop. The old-fashioned hinged tongs are better than the modern type with a spring for a hinge, though the latter are smaller and slightly easier to play. Buy four small Indian cymbals, 5 to 13cm. in diameter. If these are not available, the so-called Indian bells made for infants' schools of about 3mm. thick brass discs are cheap, although their tone does not compare with real Indian instruments. The cymbals should be matched so as to avoid a definite pitch from either pair. Each cymbal will have a definite pitch, but if it is matched with a discordant rather than a concordant pitch, the result should be sufficiently muddled to disguise this. One pair should be higher in jangling pitch than the other. (See Plate 3.)

Match the backs, the convex sides, of the cymbals to the ends of the tongs and, if necessary, file down or saw off the points of any claws so that the cymbals do not touch them. Drill a hole through the end of each arm of the tongs of a size to accommodate the rivets to be used. If necessary, reamer out the hole through the centre of each cymbal, very carefully so as not to crack the cymbals, to make a comfortably loose fit; the cymbals must not be held rigidly. Rivet one cymbal to the end of each arm of each pair of tongs, with the heads of the rivets inside the cups of the cymbals, but make sure that the rivets do not hold the cymbals rigidly in position or the tone will suffer. Small brass bolts can be used, provided that they are not screwed up tight. It is worth running solder into the threads after the nuts are in position, since otherwise they will work themselves off the bolts as the cymbals move in use.

[36]

STRING DRUM (TAMBOURIN DE BÉARN)

The lower plate on p.24 of *Early Percussion Instruments* shows the normal shape of the string drum. The number of strings varies, today being from four to ten. The box can be either built up from sheets of wood with a block inside each end to take the tuning pins and the hitch pins, or gouged from a solid bar with a separate plate for the belly. My own was gouged from a bar of deal with a cedarwood belly; a hardwood body would probably have been better but would have cost more and taken longer to make. Instruments vary in size, an average being just under 90cm. long by 18cm. wide and 7.5cm. thick. The wings on each side of the top of the instrument are traditional and help to prevent the pegs being knocked out of tune. The pegs on the instrument illustrated are viola pegs, an example that I have followed; other instruments have pegs with the older triangular tops, like crude, heavy lute pegs. A tuning hammer is essential and the strain of the thick gut strings is such that a metal one is better than wood (see fig. n). The pattern and the number of sound holes or roses vary from one instrument to another and may either be carved from the belly or made of leather or other material and inserted into the belly. The upper bridge is normally double, the smaller and higher bridge both helping the strings to turn the corner into the peg box and keeping the strings high on the shanks of the pegs.

Fig. n
Tuning hammer made of brass bar for the tambourin de Béarn

The larger of the two upper bridges has a stepped profile (fig. o). The flat ledge on the side furthest from the tuning pegs carries a set of heavy metal staples, one passing over each string. The staples are made of brass or iron wire about 2mm. in thickness and must be adjusted so that they just touch the string. The string buzzes against them, producing a loud, rich sound. They very easily go out of adjustment and an advantage of a metal tuning hammer is that it can also be used on these staples.

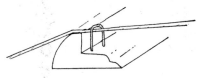

Fig. o
Profile of the main bridge on the tambourin de Béarn, showing the metal
staple against which the string buzzes

Only two gauges of string are normally used, the instrument being
tuned to the tonic and dominant of the pipe. The heavier gauges of string
used for snare gut seem to work adequately; plain cello strings would be
an alternative. The lower ends of the strings can be secured to heavy
hitch pins, or holes can be drilled right through the bottom of the
instrument and the strings knotted on the far side. The lower bridge is
similar to the uppermost of the top bridges.

FRICTION DRUM (ROMMELPOT)

Pots such as earthenware seven-pound jam-jars or medium stew pots are
ideal, but any pot or jug with a well-pronounced rim will do. The head
should be stout drum skin. The stick should be of sufficiently hard wood
not to drive splinters into the fingers; beech dowel about 1cm. thick is
suitable.

Make a groove round one end of the stick, 1cm. or so from one end,
and as deep as is safe without the stick breaking. Soak the skin as usual
and put the stick in the centre, the smooth side of the skin to the stick.
Fold the skin round the end of the stick, keeping the folds in the skin as
small as possible and tie it really hard into the groove with cord. There
will be a strong pull on the stick and it must not be able to come out of
this pocket. Put the skin over the pot, stick outwards, and tie it fairly
firmly under the rim. Pull the skin through the tie, keeping the pulls even
so that the stick remains at the centre of the skin, getting rid of as many
of the folds in the skin as possible so that there are no creases in the head.
Continue until the stick is standing upright. Either tie another cord round
under the rim, tying it down really hard so that the skin cannot slacken
itself, or fold the skin back over the first tie and tie it down again. Trim

off any excess fringe but leave enough to pull on if it needs to be reset. Leave for twenty-four hours to dry. The stick is well rubbed with beeswax or a similar substance to make it sticky so that it does not slide smoothly through the fingers, which must judder along it.

SHOE CLAPPERS (SCABELLUM)

At the time of writing, shoes with thick wooden soles and heels are fashionable in Britain. It would be easy to drill out a compartment for timbrel jingles or other rattles, or to saw through heel or sole and refix with a hinge to form a flap. When such shoes are not available, a co-operative cobbler could build a false sole and heel on to normal footwear.

BONES AND SPOONS

Beef rib bones are the best for clappers. Most butchers will still sell a rib of beef on the bone and, since at least two and probably four rib bones are required, this is one of the most enjoyable instruments to make. Those with smaller appetites, or purses, should ask their butcher to keep some bones for the next time they call. Ask for the full length of the rib. The bones must be boiled and scrubbed until they are no longer greasy.

Leg bones can be struck against each other or against a skull. Direct access to a slaughterhouse may be necessary to get a skull, though the butcher may be able to help through his market contacts. The traditional way of cleaning a skull is by burying it in an ant heap. Horse bones may be obtained through a pet-food shop. In all cases, explain exactly what is required and why it is wanted; otherwise the butcher will chop the bones up into pieces in order to be helpful.

Ordinary dessertspoons, usually of fairly thick metal, are used by street buskers today. In other parts of Europe, wooden spoons carved from boxwood or similar hard woods are specially made for musical purposes. One can buy box or olive wood salad spoons which should work well. Picken reports that in Turkey wooden spoons are boiled in olive-oil for five or ten minutes, allowed to drain and are then hardened in air for at least twenty-four hours before use. This treatment is said to improve the tone. Teaspoons will be too small and tablespoons may be too large; within those limits, try whatever there is in the kitchen drawer.

POUNDING STAVE AND JINGLING JOHNNIE

Cut a stave of wood, 4 or 5cm. thick, long enough to come to shoulder height from the ground. Set the bottom of the stave into an iron ferrule or shoe to protect it. Because a concert hall may object to having little dents hammered into its platform and a church to its floor tiles being cracked, it is sensible to carry a thick block of wood on which to pound the stave. The jingles are any old bits of iron: rings, bent nails, lengths of harness or plough chain, each separately stapled into the upper part of the stave. Heavy fencing staples can be used or a nail can be hammered in half way and then bent over.

The Jingling Johnnie, Turkish Crescent, or Chinese Hat is a much more sophisticated instrument. At the top of a wooden stave is fixed a brass crescent moon, from the convex side of which hang small pellet bells; below this is a sheet metal cone in the shape of a Chinese coolie's hat with pellet bells hanging from its rim; below that again, two arms curve out-wards with pellet bells hanging from them. All these features are mounted on collars, and not directly on to the wood, and all the collars fit sufficiently loosely to clatter up and down when the stave is moved. There is a wide range of variation in the design of these features and some instruments have small brass clapper bells, true bells, instead of pellet bells. There may also be horse-hair plumes on the ends of the arms. These instruments were used in the German and French armies within this century and examples can often be found in antique or old instrument shops. They are not uncommon in museums so that it would not be difficult to make an exact copy of an original instrument. Small brass clapper bells can be bought in ironmongers in French market towns; they are still in common use as animal bells. Sources of pellet bells have been suggested on p.33. The rest of the instrument would probably need to be made by specialist metal workers. (See Plate 2.)

TIMPANI

It is not suggested that players should build their own timpani. One might be able to find a pair of small cavalry drums or one of the small drum-making firms which still exist could make a pair. If a pair is to be made, it would be worth visiting one of the museums, such as that in Prague, which have collections of early timpani, and taking exact measurements. Some fairly typical sizes are: 57 and 59cm. diameters by 31cm. deep, or even as small as 47cm. and 49.5cm. diameters by 24cm. deep; it was normal for both drums of a pair to be the same depth. The early renaissance timpani seem to have been even smaller, perhaps 38 and 40.5cm. in diameter. (See Plate 4.)

The heads were lapped directly on to the iron counter hoops, which are therefore both counter and flesh hoops. The technique for lapping is as described above on p.15, except that it is necessary to cut small slits in the head so that the brackets for the tuning screws can project through the skin. Normally a reverse lap is used, done by laying the skin down with the smooth side uppermost before placing the hoop on it; one needs to allow about 1.5cm. more collar all round for this technique, which has the advantage that the hoop does not project above the rim of the drum. Make sure that the skin is lapped just as far round the hoop as it will go, so that it binds securely. The reverse lap is a little more difficult to do than the ordinary lap but it is better when there is no separate counter hoop or where, as on modern pedal drums, the counter hoop is L shaped.

All timpani have an air hole at the apex of the bowl. Many of the early timpani have a metal funnel, looking like a small trumpet or french horn bell, fixed round this hole and projecting up into the bowl. Nothing like enough research has been done into these, but it is obvious that they must have had a considerable effect upon the tone. Unfortunately, we do not know how the size and shape of the funnel should relate to the size of the drum, nor do we know how far they should project up into the shell. Some research and experiment are badly needed on these. What we do know is that from the middle of the seventeenth to the middle of the eighteenth century, and possibly both earlier and later, they were usually fitted, and this should be borne in mind when designing reconstructions.

Early timpani either have no stands at all or else have three small feet, just sufficient to raise the base of the bowl from the ground, for storage. For performance, one needs stands. The simplest and most easily adjustable in height are made as follows. Take four bolts 9mm. in diameter and 7 or 8cm. long. Saw off their heads and lay them down flat with their head ends together to form a plus sign. Weld the heads together, making sure that the bolts stay flat and at 90° to each other. Take four lengths of 2.5cm. dowel, 75cm. long, and four 75cm. lengths of aluminium tubing which will accept the dowel as an exact fit. Push the dowel into the tubing and drill a 1cm. diameter hole through the exact midpoint of each length. Put one arm of the four-armed bolt through each hole and fit a washer and wing-nut to each. The extent to which the stand opens, and thus the height of the drums, is controlled by adjusting the wing-nuts. Rubber ferrules, such as are fitted to crutches, should be fitted to each end of each tube to protect the floor and to prevent passers-by from scraping themselves. A similar stand is useful for the large side drum; longer legs will be needed for a larger drum. The wooden dowel can be used without the aluminium tubing, but the stands will then be much less strong; the two together form a stressed skin construction. (See Plate 4.)

Orchestral players normally play seated on stools. It is more traditional to play standing and, if the elaborate crossing of sticks technique described in *Early Percussion Instruments* is cultivated, this will show to greater advantage at the back of the orchestra if the player stands.

XYLOPHONE

We do not know what sort of wood was used for the early renaissance xylophone. Any wood will produce notes of definite pitch, and any hard wood has a better tone than a soft wood. The material used today, Honduras rosewood, was unknown in Europe before the beginning of the nineteenth century; mahogany was only imported from the beginning of the eighteenth century. Mersenne, in the middle of the seventeenth century, suggests 'a resonant wood, such as beech, or whatever wood one wishes'. This suggests that there was no uniformity and that one could use whatever wood was most convenient. If this is so, there seems no great harm in converting an instrument.

One can sometimes pick up old orchestral xylophones of late nine-teenth- or early twentieth-century date with bars of almost square section which are not hollowed out underneath; the modern rectangular section bars, which are hollowed underneath, like an arch, must not be used because their tone is much deeper. The upper surface of the bars may be rounded, so that the end of the bar looks like a squarish D on its side, but the upper and lower surfaces of the bar must not be more than a very little wider than the bar is deep. The function of the arched hollow below the bar on the modern xylophone is to flatten the pitch and to improve the tone. The resulting sound, good though it is for the modern orchestra, is completely wrong for an early xylophone. Also wrong for our purposes are the modern methods of tuning the bars, all of which improve the tone. The only methods which can be allowed are a shallow saw cut across the width of the centre of the underside of the bar to flatten the pitch and cutting small pieces off the ends of the bar to sharpen it.

Another possible source for the bars is one of the instruments made for school use, many of which have a range of a twelfth, diatonic or chromatic, which is all that is required, and many of which have bars of the early pattern. The bars may need to be tuned; few of the cheaper school instruments are in tune, either to concert pitch or within themselves.

Alternatively, one can buy 2.5cm. square section rods of hardwood, or 2.5cm. diameter beech dowel, and make bars. The pitch of a xylophone bar depends upon its length, thickness (not width, which affects only its tone), and density. As no piece of wood is of equal density down its length, one cannot plan the lay-out in advance; start by sawing off a bar about 25cm. long and work in both directions from there. If one bar comes out too sharp, it can be shortened and used for the next note up. If a cylindrical rod is used, it will be essential to fix it in such a way that it cannot revolve on its axis; this could change the pitch. A xylophone bar will only sound when supported at its nodal points, approximately two-ninths from each end. The exact spots can be found by sprinkling french chalk or fine sand on the bar and tapping it until the chalk collects in two little piles at the nodes. The traditional supporting material was hanks of straw; raffia such as is used for lamp shades would make an adequate substitute, tied in tight bundles 1cm. or so in diameter. The hanks can be stapled to the frame, which will either be a simple ladder or a double ladder, depending upon whether the instrument is to be diatonic or chromatic. Make the bars before the frame, because the hanks of straw must come precisely under the nodal points of the bars and these cannot be established until the lengths of the bars are known. Lay the bars on the straw, the diatonic instrument in a straight row, with B flat coming between the A and the B natural, the chromatic either in a double row with the 'black' notes in their usual keyboard places, or with the bars arranged in the same pattern as the strings of the chromatic dulcimer, for which the xylophone was a substitute. In this last pattern, the bars were arranged in three, or sometimes even four interlocking rows so that the right-hand nodal points of the left-hand row rested on the same straw as the left-hand nodes of the central row, and the left-hand nodal points of the right-hand row shared the straw with the right-hand nodes of the central row. Tie each bar down with a piece of string round the bar and under the straw. Only the diatonic xylophone which was hung from a nail in the wall, like that illustrated by Mersenne, normally had the bars pierced for a cord like our modern instruments. When making this pattern, follow Mersenne's advice and place a small rosary bead on the cord between each bar to hold them apart. The bars should be pierced exactly at the nodal points, though the holes may run through the width of the bars on a diagonal line, starting fractionally to one side of the nodal point and coming out fractionally to the other side, in order to keep the suspension cord in a straight line. This type of xylophone will be inconvenient to play, since there is no frame and the player depends upon the nail from which it hangs to keep it in position. Remember that although the modern xylophone is played from the side, the older instruments were always played from the end with the longest bars, the bars running across the body instead of away from it as today. The modern pattern of xylophone is quite inappropriate.

There are many forms of dulcimer and it is suggested that, before making one, it would be sensible to visit a museum and see what sort is most suitable, and then copy that. The basic construction is quite simple. Two bars of hardwood are needed for the sides of the instrument, one to take the tuning pins and the other the hitch pins. These are laid down with their further ends closer together than the nearer ends, resembling the legs of an A below the cross bar. The body is made by gluing a sheet of hardwood, such as maple, underneath them to form the back and a sheet of softwood, such as spruce, across the top to form the sound-board.

A front board and a back board are inserted to fill the gaps and to hold the sides apart against the pull of the strings. The soundboard should have one or more sound holes cut in it, which are customarily filled with a rose. The strings are arranged in courses of three or four to each note and the tuning and hitch pins are set in line with each other in a diagonal, sufficient to keep the strings of each course together but not touching each other. Allow space enough between each course to distinguish between them when playing. A good piano supply house will produce harpsichord tuning pins, a tuning key to fit them, and wire for the strings. For the earlier instruments, brass wire will be more authentic than iron wire. Experiment will be needed to determine what gauge and tension of string will best suit any particular size of instrument. A tension about a whole tone below the breaking point gives the best tone, though a third below is more economical on wire.

The position of the bridges will depend upon whether the instrument is diatonic or chromatic. Diatonic instruments had one bridge down each side, just on the soundboard, either a plain bar or an arcaded bar, as in Mersenne's illustration. The bridges will need to be pinned, like a harpsi-chord bridge, so that the strings have something to bear against. The third bridge of the chromatic instruments was either one third of the way across the soundboard, to produce a note and its octave, or two-fifths of the way, to produce a note and its fifth. Other arrangements are also found, the basic idea being that an instrument with a chromatic compass of a twelfth or two octaves would be too wide from front to back for comfort if it had a separate course for each note. The third bridge was often made in separate pieces, each piece resembling a rook or a pawn from a chess set, and carrying one course.

The Chinese instruments today have a small drawer, set into the front board, to take the beaters and tuning key, and this is an idea worth copying, even though anachronistic; beaters are light and fragile and easily lost.

LONG DRUM

The construction is exactly the same as the large side drum, allowing for the differences in the dimensions, with counter hoops as well as flesh hoops. Typical sizes are 45 to 60cm. in diameter and 60 to 90cm. in depth. Suspension was either by a ring, screwed through the exact centre of the shell into a block, with a harness going over the player's shoulders and chest clipped into the ring, or by a strap secured to each end of the shell like the large tabors and passing behind the player's neck.

A stand for orchestral use can be made by fixing four pieces of timber together to make two Xs and joining them with a bar fixed to the crossing point of each X. The upper jaws of each X should be padded to support the drum and the cross-bar should be of such a length that the Xs support the drum just inside the flesh hoops, so that the drum does not slip off the stand. A piece of knobbed rubber on the bottom of each length will help to prevent the stand from moving. The stand should hold the centre of the drum heads at chest height; if it is too low, it will be very tiring to play.

6

CARE AND MAINTENANCE

No drum is complete until it has a cover for its heads and no instrument is ready for use until it has a case. The player who travels to every concert and rehearsal by car may be satisfied with a soft case or bag, sufficient to keep off the rain, but those who travel by any form of public transport must have some form of rigid protection for all the instruments.

Covers can be made from discs of hardboard with a sheet of plastic foam glued to the rough side. Before fixing the foam, drill pairs of holes 2 or 3 cm. from the edge, north and south or north, south, east, and west, and insert a cord in each pair of holes, the free ends coming out of the smooth side of the hardboard and long enough to tie under the Vs of the tension cords or the brackets of the tuning handles of the timpani. Each cover should be marked with the name of the drum it belongs to and, for the drums with a snare, which head, for the snare will make itself a bed in the foam. A similar cover should be made for the xylophone and dulcimer so that if they are slid into a box, the bars and strings are not scraped.

Trapezium-shaped boxes can be made for xylophone and dulcimer, with the 'front board' hinged so that the instrument can be slid in; this is a slightly stronger construction than a hinged lid.

Professional drum shops can make, or have made, fibre cases for the drums. When ordering, allow width for the snare pegs or these will have to be removed in transit and the first hour of any rehearsal be spent continually adjusting the snares as they settle down. Allow space also for a lining of foam; the drums will not always be under the player's eye and may be dropped by porters. Small instruments can be carried in a case of their own, as can beaters, or one or more compartments for accessories can be built into a larger case. I have had separate cases made for all the larger instruments and for the nakers as well as one large box, which can just be carried with one hand. This is for the timbrels, small tabors, and small side drum, both pairs of nakers which fit in in their own cases one above the other, and accessories in two compartments, one each side of the nakers. Fig. p shows the layout, in case this should be useful to others. The larger odds and ends, such as cymbals, which are not often used, live in an old suitcase with the reserve stock of beaters.

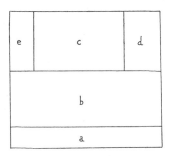

Fig. p Plan for a large multiple drum case
(a) two timbrels side by side; (b) small tabors and side drum; (c) two pairs of nakers in their own cases, one above the other; (d) triangle, wrist pellet bells, cymbals; (e) beaters

All the parts of every instrument should be checked at least once a year; tension cords, buffs, suspension straps, and everything that might be getting worn or frayed. Tension screws on the timpani, and the screws which hold the timpani stands, should be greased also at least once a year. Always check all drum heads and snares a day or two before any rehearsal; these can go of their own accord and it is no use arriving at rehearsal or concert with a broken drum. It takes thirty-six hours to fit a new head, allowing for drying time, so do not leave this check until the last minute. It is sensible always to have some spare heads in stock; it is precisely at times of emergency that one's normal suppliers run out of stock.

It is sensible, also, to have spare beaters in reserve. When buying beaters, always buy more than are needed. The next batch, whether months or years later, are always different and it is never possible to match beaters exactly from one batch to another.

REFERENCES

A full bibliography will be found in *Early Percussion Instruments*. Those books which have been specifically mentioned in this book are listed below.

Our only evidence for percussion instruments earlier than the 16th century is in the pictorial arts of each place and time. Therefore it is essential to look at picture books, at the books on the art of the relevant areas and periods, at the illustrated histories of music, at art galleries, at carvings in churches, and at every source we can find. If we take the task of reconstructing early percussion instruments seriously, we must build up illustration archives and we must catalogue and index them in such a way that we can find what we need. Look always at the postcard stalls in museums, and buy any that show early percussion instruments; keep an eye on Christmas cards; look out for music publishers' illustrated calendars. All this material swells the archives and, so often, there is just one picture which has the information which we need for a particular instrument. Only with some system such as that designed by Brown and Lascelle can we hope to find that picture in reasonable time.

ARBEAU, THOINOT. *Orchésographie* (Langres, 1589); various editions in English, the latest being Dover Press, New York, 1967; reprint, Minkoff, Geneva, 1972.

BROWN, HOWARD MAYER and JOAN LASCELLE. *Musical Iconography: a manual for cataloguing musical subjects in Western art* (Harvard Univ. Press, Cambridge, Mass., 1972).

MERSENNE, MARIN. *Harmonie Universelle* (Paris, 1636); reprint Centre National de la Recherche Scientifique, Paris, 1963.

PICKEN, LAURENCE. *Folk Musical Instruments of Turkey* (Oxford Univ. Press, London, 1975).

PRAETORIUS, MICHAEL. *Syntagma Musicum* (*Volume II*, 'De Organographia') (Wolffenbüttel, 1619); reprint Bärenreiter, Kassel, 1958.